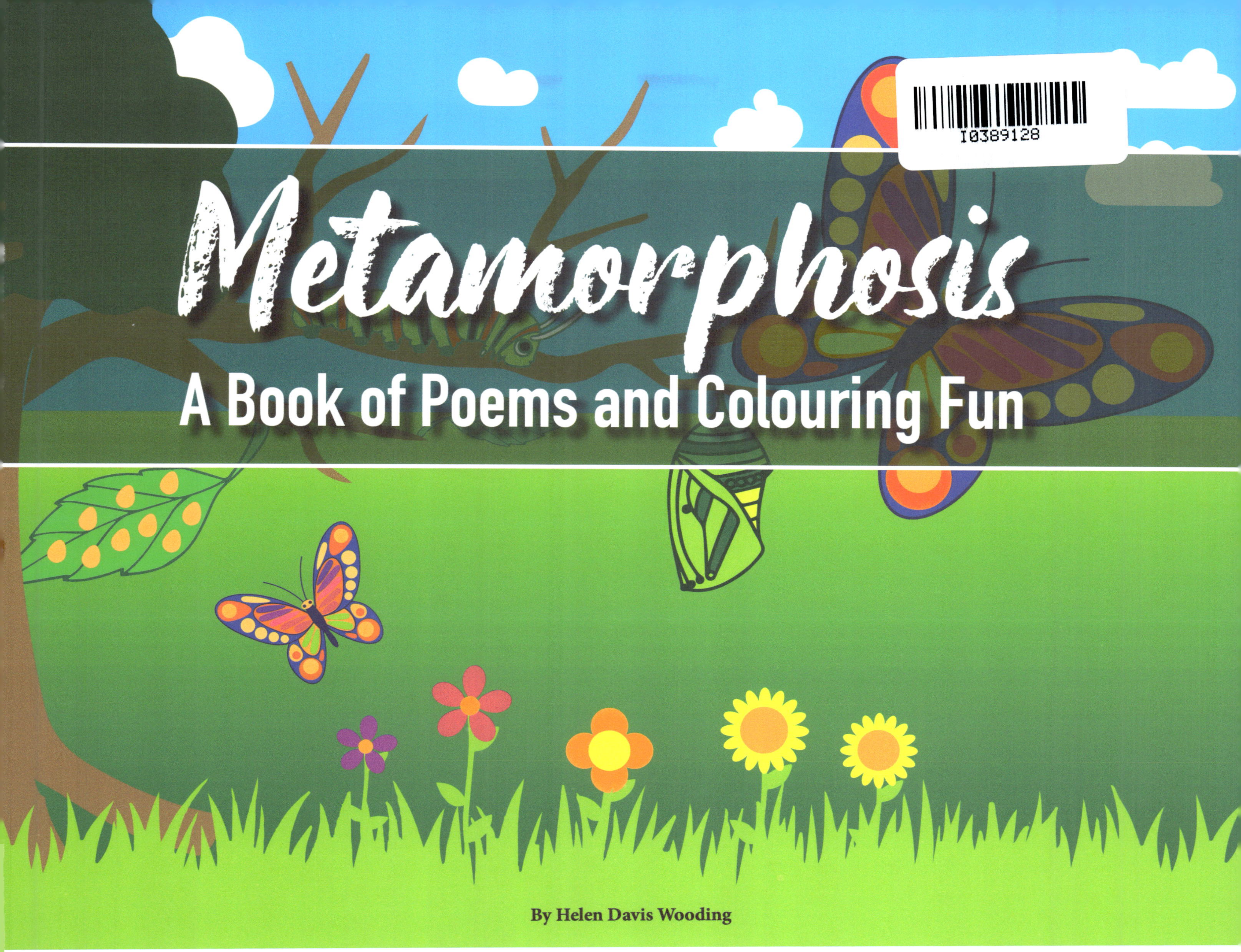

Metamorphosis
A Book of Poems and Colouring Fun

By Helen Davis Wooding

The Rainbow

See the rainbow in the sky,
Makes an arch,
Oh so high!
How many colours do you see?
I see seven,
Can you count with me?
What are the colours?
Do you know?
Sure, I do,
Ready, set, go!

Red, violet, blue, yellow,
Orange, green and indigo.
Who put them there?
Why is it so?
It's a sign from God to show,
He'll never again,
Flood the earth below.

The Rosebud

A Poem for Parents

The rosebud
Is the 'young' of the rose,
Its soft and delicate petals
Forming as they grow.
Needing careful nurturing,
As it imperceptibly unfolds,
Gracefully maturing, into the
Perfect rose.

Should anyone force its petals open,
Through ignorance or
Lack of patience,
What would become of the rose-to-be?
Nothing the eye would want to see.

So carefully consider,
As you compare
The rosebud, to the child.
Growing and developing,
Maturing and blossoming,
The perfect rose,
The perfect blossoming of the child.

Metamorphosis
To the Beat of Your Drums

Caterpillar crawling
 with many legs and eyes,
Hatched from the egg
 of a mother butterfly.

Attaches itself
 to the branch of a tree,
Neatly spinning a cocoon,
 its hiding place to be.

Getting ready to change,
 to metamorphosize,
Emerging elegantly,
 as a pretty butterfly.

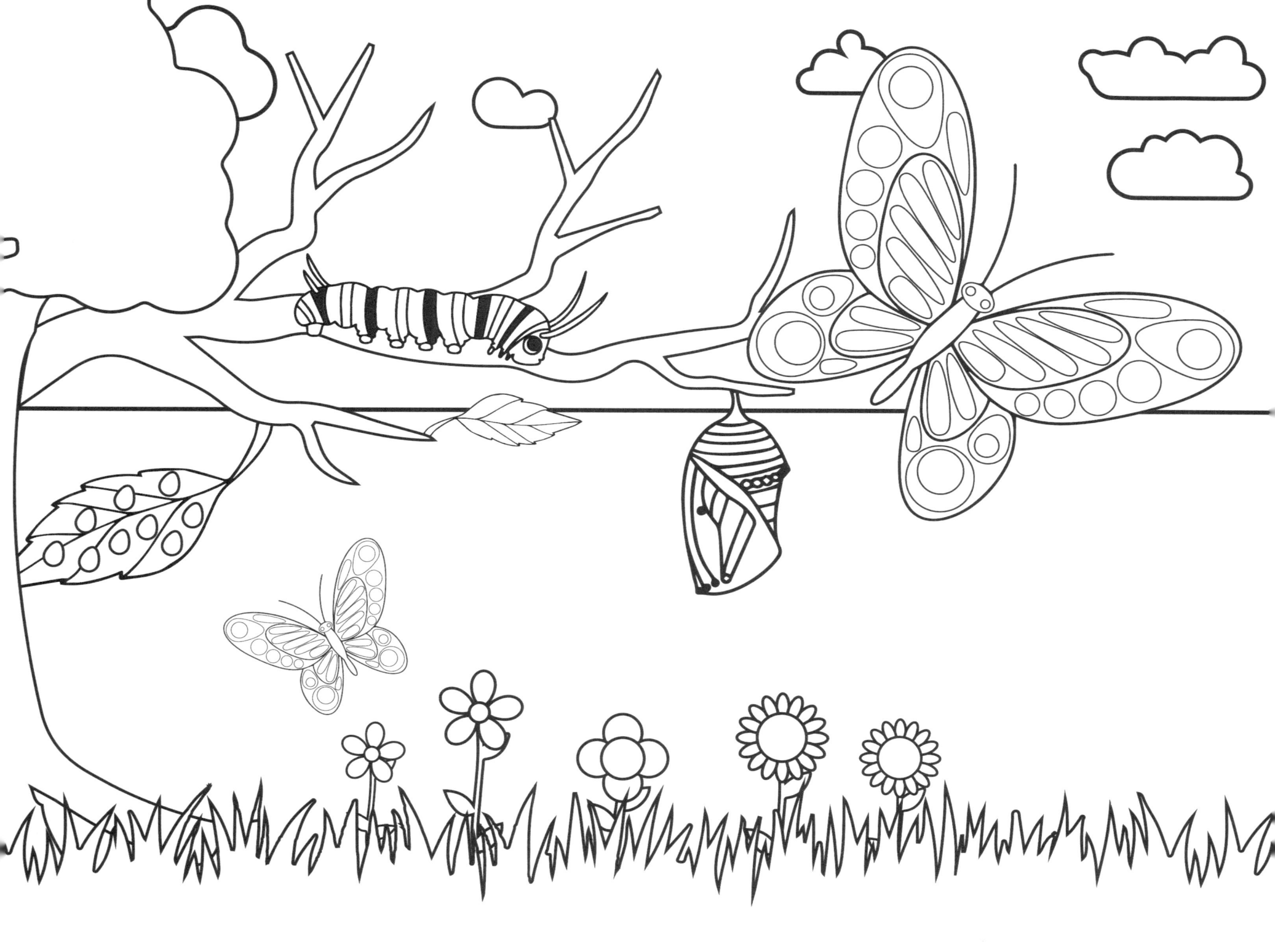

God's Creation

All things in creation sing;
God made all things.
He made the day,
He made the night,
When He said,
"Let there be light!"
He made the heavens,
Oh, so high!
In a place
He called the sky.
He made the lands,
He made the seas,
He made the grass,
The plants and trees.
He made the stars
That shine so bright,
The sun and moon
To give us light.
He made the fish
That love to swim.
He made the birds
That love to sing.
He made all animals,
Insects and beasts.
Then made Man,
Last but not least.
He breathed life into
His nose,
And man became a
Living soul.

I Am An Ambassador

I am an Ambassador,
Because of who I am,
Respecting my Creator,
My God, the great I AM!

I am an Ambassador,
To a nation I belong,
Being a good example
To the nations all around.

I am an Ambassador,
In a family God placed me,
Honouring my father and mother,
I am building community.

I am an Ambassador,
Representing my school well,
With character as my uniform,
I am able to excel.

An Ambassador for God,
To the nations of the earth,
Thankful for my family,
And valuable lessons learnt.

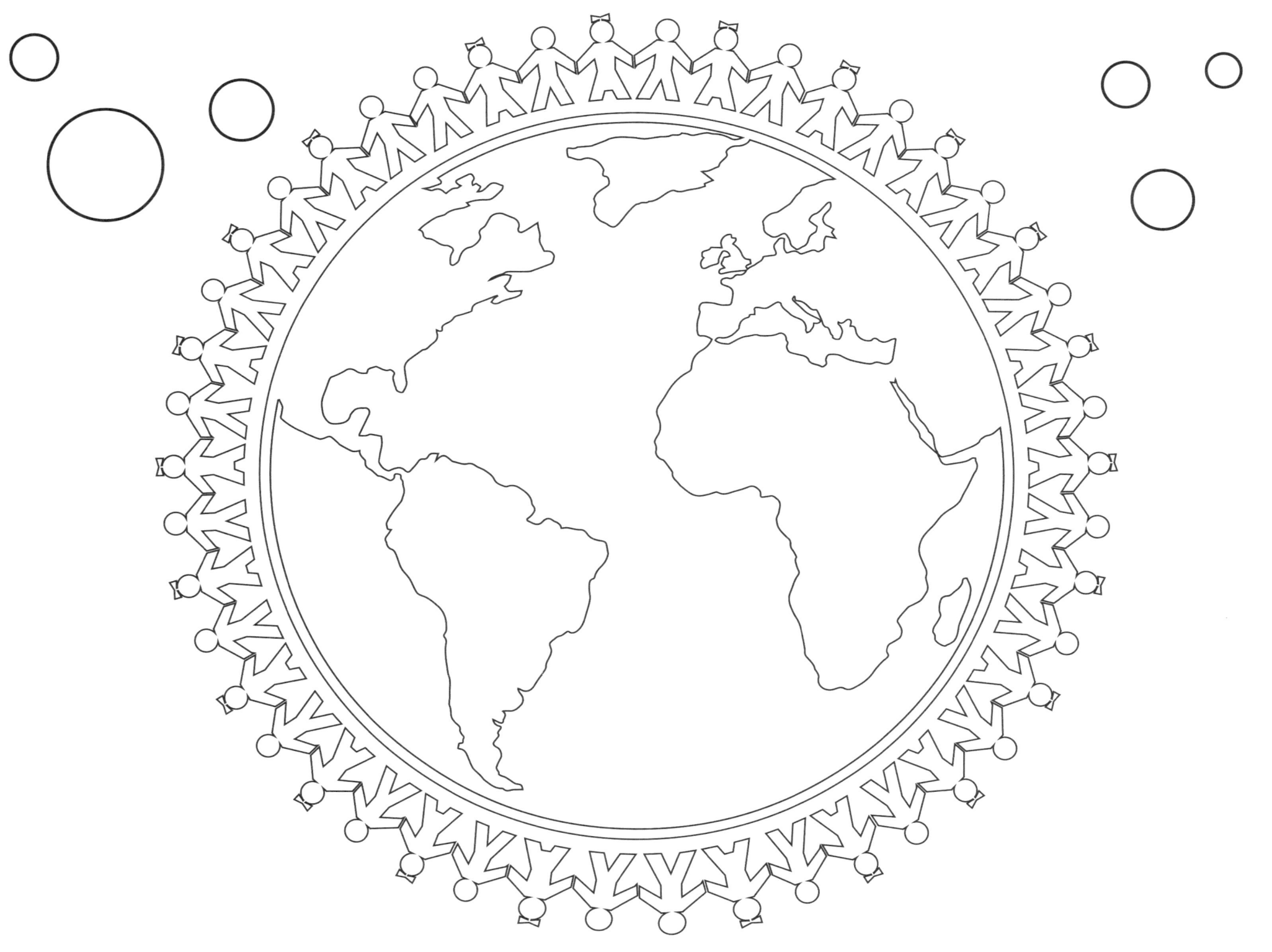

Land, Sea, Air & Space

Land, Sea, Air and Space,
Ways to go from place to place,
Land, Sea, Air and Space,
Travel for the human race.

To travel by land,
We can walk or ride,
A camel, horse or on a bike.
Jump on a train or drive a car,
When we must travel very far.

To travel by sea,
We sail in ships,
Row kayaks and canoes
As some sailors wish.
Or row with oars in a dinghy,
While captains steer submarines
Under the sea.

Travel to space,
Is a very long trip,
Zooming through the universe
In rockets and ships.
I would like to be
An astronaut one day,
Visiting planets far away!

Land, Sea, Air and Space,
Travel for the human race,
Land, Sea, Air and Space,
It's fun to travel from place to place.

It's A Wonderful World

It's a wonderful world
created by God
The shape of a sphere
like a giant beach ball
Spinning on its axis
not causing us to fall
It's a beautiful, wonderful
world!

It's a wonderful world
of lands and seas
Where people live
in communities
From East to West
and North to South
It's a beautiful, wonderful
world!

It's a wonderful world,
Let's communicate
Near or far,
We don't have to wait
Talk, text, call!
Send a long email
It's a beautiful, wonderful
world!

God in heaven,
Not far away
So I can reach Him
Whenever I pray
Anytime, whether night or day
It's a beautiful, wonderful
world!

I Wonder

I look in the mirror
And what do I SEE?
I see my body
Looking back at me.
I twist and I turn,
I look and I learn,
And wonder,
"WHO made me?
Who put me in my body?"

I run to my parents
And what do I HEAR?
"God made your body
And put you in there".
I jump up and down,
I spin all around,
And wonder,
"HOW do I care
 For my body?"

I am called to dinner
And what do I SMELL?
Flavours of food
That I cannot tell.
I look and I guess,
I thank and I bless,
And wonder,
"WHICH foods are best
For my body?"

I sit at the table
And what do I TASTE?
Carrots and pumpkin,
Channa and chicken.
I sit in my seat,
I give thanks and eat,
And wonder,
"WHERE does food go
When it enters my body?

I lean back in my chair
And what do I TOUCH?
My full belly now,
A heaping stomach.
That's all I can eat,
So I jump to my feet
And wonder,
"HOW else can I care
For my body?"

RESPECT

(Sung to the tune of the ABC song)

R-E-S-P-E-C-T
What does this word mean to me?
Take one letter at a time,
Seven words and make them
Rhyme.

R-E-S-P-E-C-T
See what this word means to me.

Show **R**ESPONSIBILITY,
When I'm sad, **E**NCOURAGE me,
SHARE with me
And be **P**OLITE.
Be an **E**XAMPLE, do what's right.
Think of me, **C**ONSIDER me,
TEAM together and work with me.

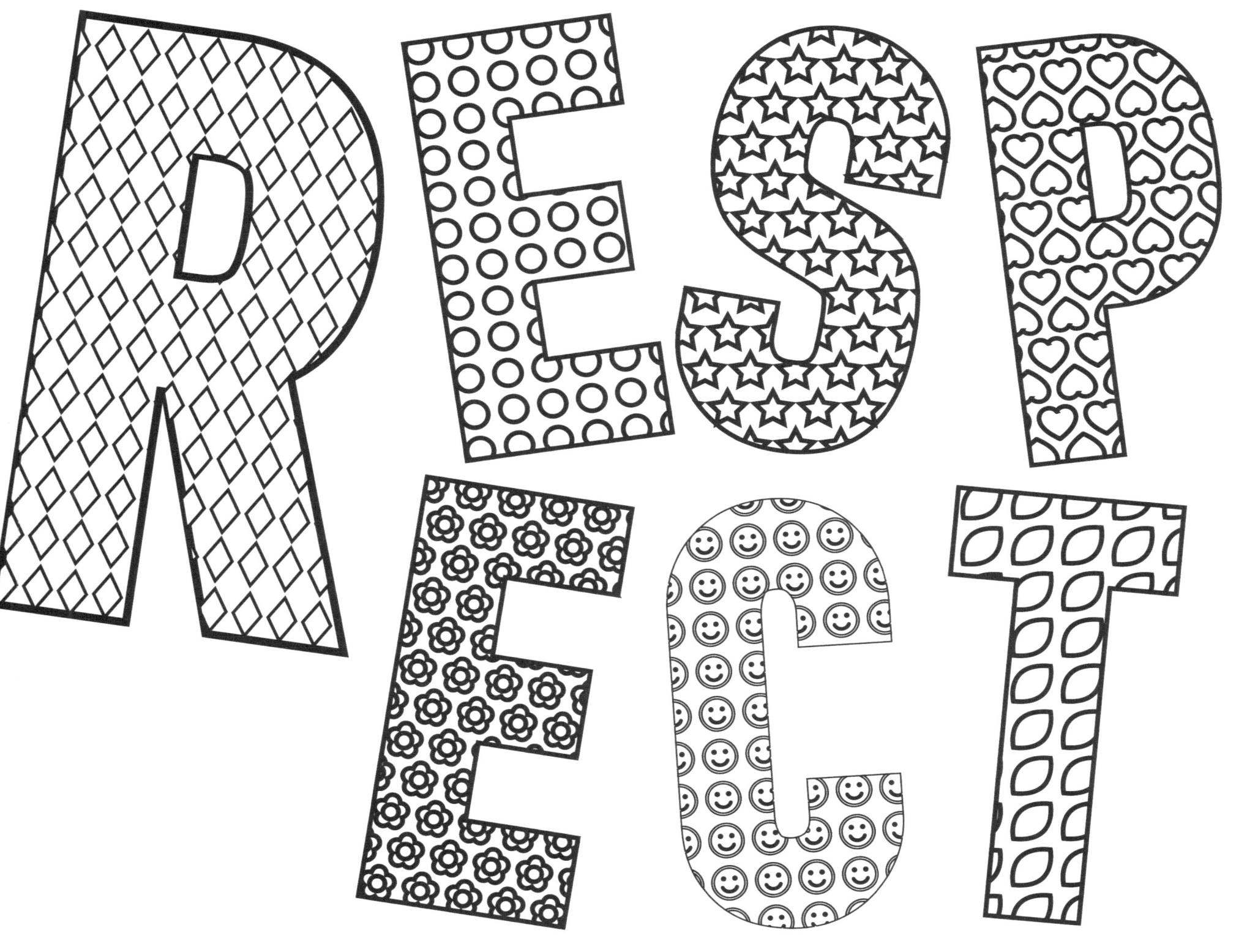

www.ingramcontent.com/pod-product-compliance
Lightning Source LLC
Chambersburg PA
CBHW042110090526
44592CB00004B/80